Super Sea Creatures

STINGRAYS

GAIL TERP

BLACK RABBIT BOOKS

Bolt is published by Black Rabbit Books
P.O. Box 227, Mankato, Minnesota, 56002.
www.blackrabbitbooks.com

Marysa Storm, editor; Grant Gould, designer;
Omay Ayres, photo researcher

Names: Terp, Gail, 1951- author.
Title: Stingrays / by Gail Terp.
Description: Mankato, Minnesota : Black Rabbit Books, [2021] | Series: Bolt. super sea creatures | Includes bibliographical references and index. | Audience: Ages 8-12 | Audience: Grades 4-6 | Summary: "Dive into learning about stingrays with vibrant photography, engaging text, and range maps, size comparisons, and other infographics"– Provided by publisher. Identifiers: LCCN 2019026677 (print) | LCCN 2019026678 (ebook) | ISBN 9781623102876 (hardcover) | ISBN 9781644663837 (paperback) | ISBN 9781623103811 (ebook)
Subjects: LCSH: Stingrays–Juvenile literature.
Classification: LCC QL638.8 .T47 2021 (print) | LCC QL638.8 (ebook) | DDC 597.3/5-dc23
LC record available at https://lccn.loc.gov/2019026677
LC ebook record available at https://lccn.loc.gov/2019026678

Printed in the United States.

Image Credits

Age Fotostock: W. Gregory Brown, 32; Alamy: Helmut Corneli, Cover; Reinhard Dirscherl, 4–5; WaterFrame, 28–29; Dreamstime: Rafael Ben Ari, 1; greatyarmouthmercury.co.uk, Great Yarmouth Sea Life Centre, 22; iStock: busypix, 18; Don Miller, 12; Marcos Schonholz, 15; Minden: Franco Banfi, 8–9; Fred Bavendam, 3; Georgette Douwma, 22–23; Jordi Chias, 6–7; NOAA: Dave Vendettouli, 27; Shutterstock: Anton Peichev, 24 (worms); AVA Bitter, 16–17 (bkgd); Evlakhov Valeriy, 10–11; Kletr, 24 (hammerhead, fish); Lotus Images, 24 (crab); Paii VeGa, 31; Sea of Marina, 16–17 (silhouettes); serg_dibrova, 24 (stingray); sketchfab.com: rstr_tv, 24 (bull shark); twitter.com: Sea Life, 20–21
Every effort has been made to contact copyright holders for material reproduced in this book. Any omissions will be rectified in subsequent printings if notice is given to the publisher.

CONTENTS

CHAPTER 1

IN THE SEA

A stingray swims along the ocean floor. It searches for **prey** buried in the sand. Suddenly, it feels movement. Prey! It gently waves its fins. This action moves sand to uncover a crab. Quickly, the stingray grabs the crab with its teeth. Crunch!

COMPARING SIZES

	body diameter in feet / weight in pounds
roughtail stingray	about 7 feet (2 meters) up to 661 pounds (300 kilograms)
southern stingray	2.5 to 6.6 feet (.8 to 2 m) about 200 pounds (91 kg)
Atlantic stingray	1 to 2 feet (.3 to .6 m) about 11 pounds (5 kg)

Many Kinds

Stingrays are fish that live in oceans and rivers. There are about 70 kinds. Stingrays have no bones. Their bodies are made of **cartilage**.

Stingrays come in many sizes. No matter the size, they have flat, round bodies. Their bodies tend to be dull colors. Dull colors help them blend in with the sea floor.

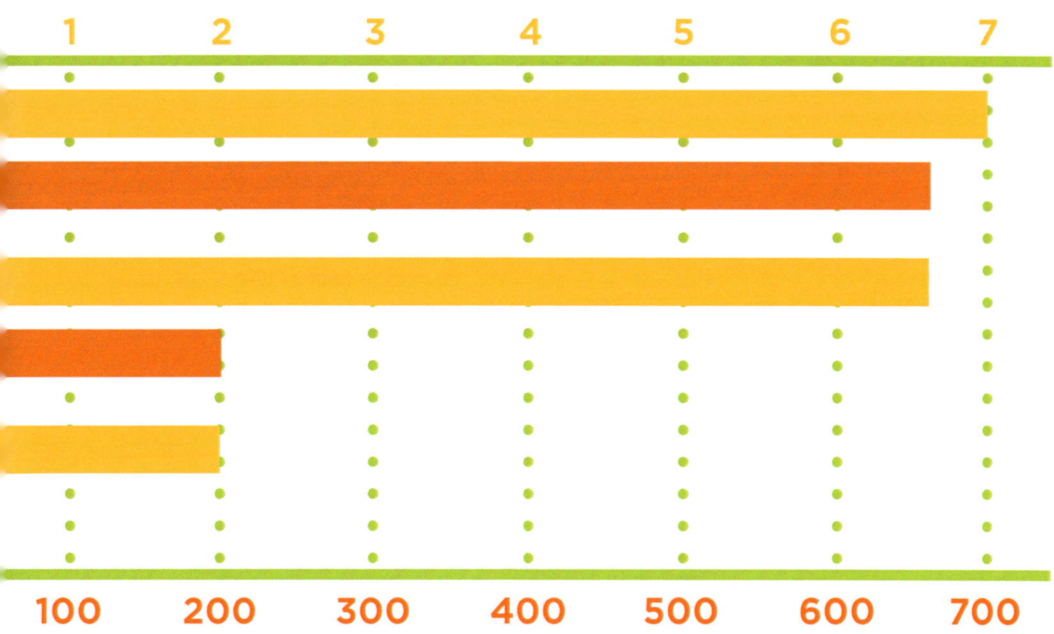

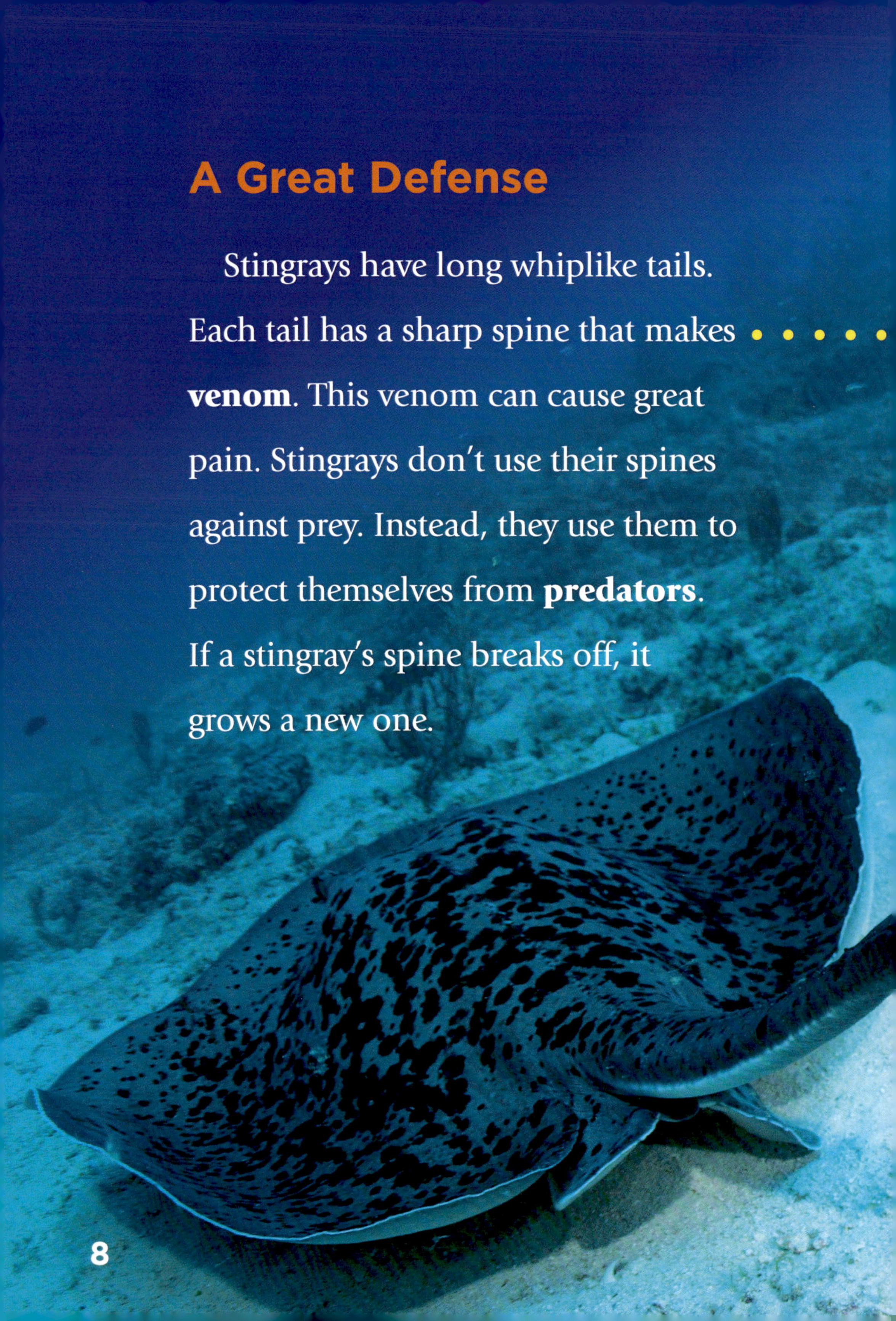

A Great Defense

Stingrays have long whiplike tails. Each tail has a sharp spine that makes **venom**. This venom can cause great pain. Stingrays don't use their spines against prey. Instead, they use them to protect themselves from **predators**. If a stingray's spine breaks off, it grows a new one.

STINGRAY FEATURES

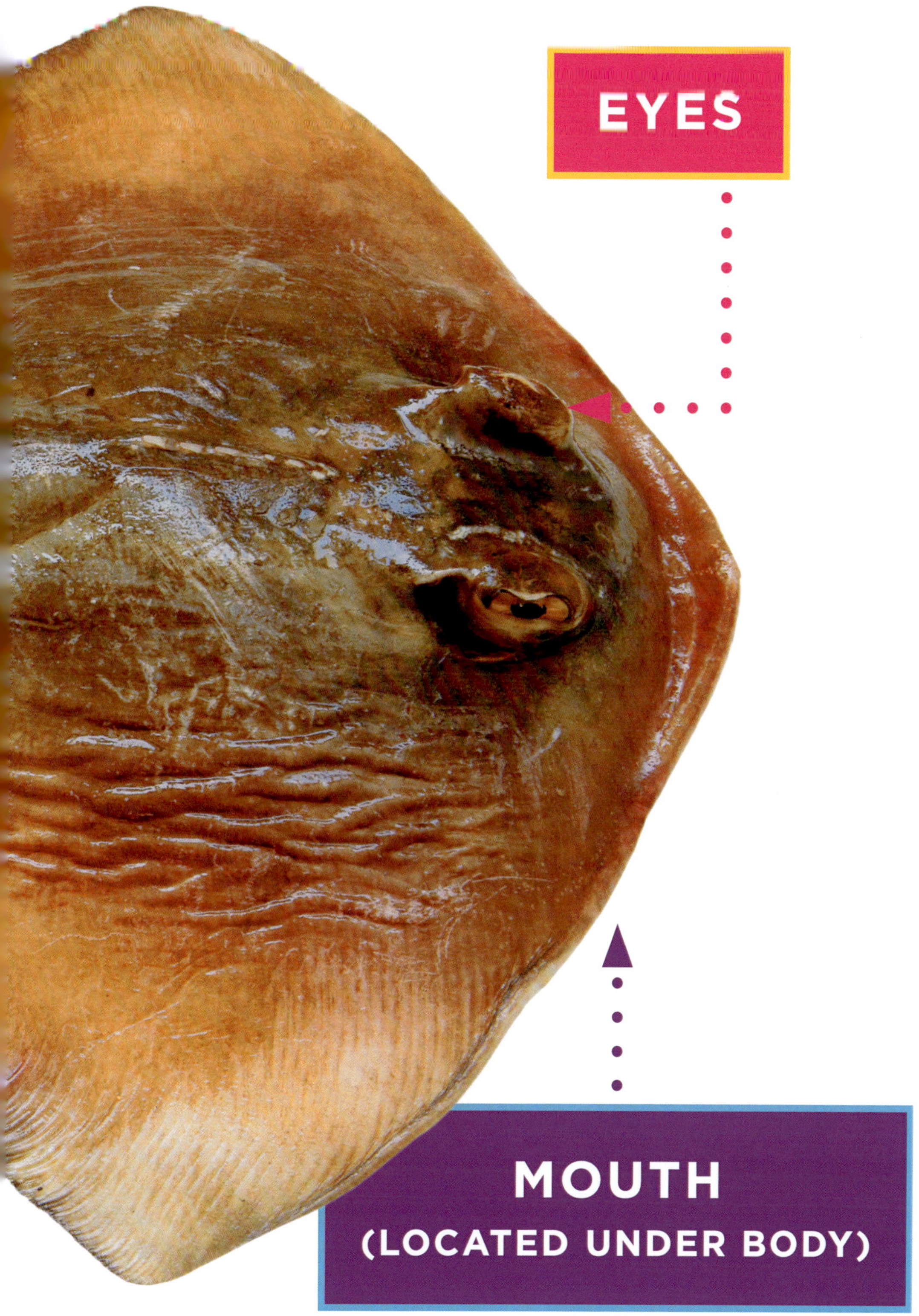
EYES
MOUTH
(LOCATED UNDER BODY)

Stingrays chew their food.

CHAPTER 2

FOOD TO EAT and a Place to Live

Stingrays eat shellfish, such as crabs and clams. They eat small fish and sea worms too. Most stingray prey is on the sea floor. It's often buried in sand. Stingrays use **sensors** around their mouths to find it. They sense electricity created by prey.

Where Stingrays Live

Most stingrays swim in oceans around the world. They tend to live in areas with warm water. Most live along **coasts**. Stingrays stay close to the sea bottom. That's where their prey is. It's a good place to hide too. Buried in sand, stingrays are hard for prey and predators to see.

There are some freshwater stingrays. They live in rivers.

WHERE SALTWATER STINGRAYS LIVE

Saltwater Stingray Range Map

CHAPTER 3

FAMILY LIFE

Some stingrays live in groups. Others live alone. Sometimes they gather to travel together. They might travel to find food or to **mate**.

All kinds of stingrays meet to mate. Each type mates once a year. The time of year stingrays mate depends on their type and location.

Babies

Up to a year after mating, female stingrays give birth. Most fish lay eggs. But stingrays have live young. The young are born ready for life at sea. They can swim and hunt. They have small spines too.

about 7 feet (2 m)
about 1 foot (.3 m)
1
2
3
4
5
6
7

BY THE NUMBERS

2 TO 10
NUMBER OF BABIES A FEMALE HAS AT ONE TIME

790 pounds
(358 kg)
WEIGHT OF LARGEST STINGRAY DISCOVERED

15 to 25 years

LIFE SPAN

up to 16 inches
(41 centimeters)
LENGTH OF SPINE

Stingray Food Chain

This food chain shows what eats stingrays. It also shows what stingrays eat.

BULL SHARKS

HAMMERHEAD SHARKS

STINGRAYS

CRABS

SMALL FISH

SEA WORMS

CHAPTER 4

Part of THEIR WORLD

Few animals eat stingrays. Most stay away because of the stingrays' size and spines. But sharks, such as bull and hammerhead sharks, hunt them. A hammerhead shark uses its wide head to pin down a stingray. Then the shark bites it.

Harmful Humans

Humans are a threat to stingrays too. They eat them and use them to make medicine. They also trap stingrays to sell to aquariums. **Pollution** and **global warming** hurt stingray habitats too.

Stingrays Are Important

Stingrays are a big part of the ocean world. They eat many animals. They're food for sharks too. Stingrays also help people. Scientists learn from them. Stingrays really are super sea creatures.

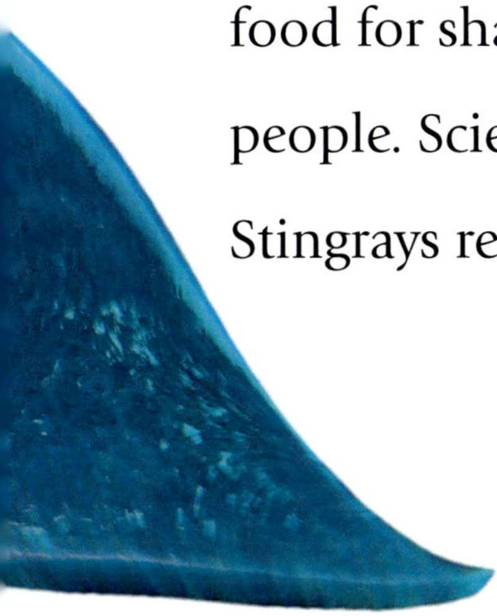

Parasites stick to stingrays. Stingrays let small fish eat the parasites.

cartilage (KAHR-tl-ij)—tough flexible tissue

coast (KOHST)—the land near a shore

global warming (GLO-buhl WARM-ing)—a warming of Earth's air and oceans

mate (MAYT)—to join together to produce young

parasite (PAR-uh-syt)—a plant or animal that lives in or on another plant or animal and gets its food or protection from it

pollution (puh-LOO-shun)—substances that make land, water, or air dirty and not safe to use

predator (PRED-uh-tuhr)—an animal that eats other animals

prey (PRAY)—an animal hunted or killed for food

sensor (SEN-sor)—something that finds heat, light, sound, motion, or other things

venom (VEH-num)—a poison made by animals used to kill or injure

LEARN MORE

BOOKS

Arnold, Quinn M. *Stingrays.* Seedlings. Mankato, MN: Creative Education/Creative Paperbacks, 2017.

McAneney, Caitie. *This Book Stings.* Beastly Books for the Brave. New York: Gareth Stevens, 2020.

Schuh, Mari. *Stingrays.* Ocean Animals. Mankato, MN: Amicus, 2020.

WEBSITES

14 Facts about Stingrays!
www.natgeokids.com/za/discover/animals/sea-life/stingray-facts/

Fun Stingray Facts for Kids
www.sciencekids.co.nz/sciencefacts/animals/stingray.html

Porcupine Ray
oceana.org/marine-life/sharks-rays/porcupine-ray

INDEX